AIR FORCE ONE

ANDREW SANTELLA

The Millbrook Press
Brookfield, Connecticut

Cover montage photographs courtesy of Getty/Archive

Photographs courtesy of San Diego Aerospace Museum: pp. 6, 17; Franklin D. Roosevelt Library: pp. 7, 9; AP/Wide World Photos: pp. 11, 12, 13, 14, 15, 24, 36, 41, 45, 46; Brown Brothers: p. 18; Harry S. Truman Library: p. 21; Cecil Stoughton, White House/John Fitzgerald Kennedy Library: p. 26; Lyndon B. Johnson Library: pp. 29, 30; © Wally McNamee/Corbis: p. 33; Ronald Reagan Library: p. 35; Getty Images: pp. 39 (Reuters/W. McNamee), 40 (Reuters).

Library of Congress Cataloging-in-Publication Data
Santella, Andrew.
Air Force One / Andrew Santella.
v. cm.
Includes bibliographical references and index.
Contents: The president's plane—The first flight—The Sacred Cow—Harry Truman's Independence—Dwight Eisenhower's Columbine—Into the jet age—John Kennedy and the new look of Air Force One—Air Force One and a day of tragedy—Lyndon Johnson's "throne"—Richard Nixon's final flight—The historic flights of SAM 27000—Twin presidential planes—Air Force One and a day of terror—Air Force One today—To learn more—Index.
ISBN 0-7613-2617-0 (lib. bdg.)   ISBN 0-7613-1926-3 (pbk.)
1. Presidential aircraft—United States—Juvenile literature. [1. Presidential aircraft.] I. Title.
TL723 .S26 2003   387.7'42'088351—dc21   2002000132

Published by The Millbrook Press, Inc.
2 Old New Milford Road
Brookfield, Connecticut 06804
www.millbrookpress.com

CONTENTS

THE FIRST FLIGHT

 ON JANUARY 11, 1943, pilot Howard Cone began preparing his airplane for a top-secret flight. Secret missions were nothing new to Cone. The United States had been fighting in World War II for just over a year, and the war had turned the Atlantic Ocean into a dangerous battlefield. Prowling German submarines threatened any ship that tried to cross the ocean. The safest way to cross was in a plane. And the only plane that could make it across was the Boeing 314 Clipper. It was the plane that Howard Cone flew.

The Clipper was the grandest airplane of its time. It could fly 3,600 miles (5,793 km) before stopping to refuel. Before the war, Clippers were used for luxurious passenger flights between Europe and the United States. But the war put an end to passenger flights. Instead, Clippers were used by the U.S. military to transport some of the most important government and military leaders in the world.

The Clipper was called a "flying boat" because it had a boatlike hull that allowed the plane to land on water.

As he prepared for his secret flight, Cone had no idea who would be traveling on his Clipper. In fact, it was only a few minutes before takeoff that Cone learned why his flight was such a secret. Nine men boarded Cone's plane in Miami on January 11. Cone recognized one of them. As soon as Cone laid eyes on the man, he understood the need for secrecy. As the man approached, Cone snapped to attention and saluted him. "Mr. President!" Cone said. "I'm glad to have you aboard, sir."

Franklin Delano Roosevelt, the thirty-second president of the United States (1933–1945), was boarding Cone's Clipper. Cone's assignment was to fly the president to North Africa for a war-planning meeting with British leader

ABOARD THE CLIPPERS

Before World War II, passengers aboard Clipper flying boats flew in luxury. They ate fine meals in the plane's elegant dining room. They settled down to sleep in special compartments outfitted with beds. They chatted with each other in the plane's barroom. It

This historic flight in 1943 made Roosevelt (left) the first president to fly while in office. Here, he sits with the captain in charge of the flight.

Winston Churchill. If the enemy found out the president was taking to the air, his plane would make an ideal target. In fact, some of the president's advisers were so worried about his safety that they thought he should stay at home. But Roosevelt insisted on making the flight. America was fighting a great global war, he told his advisers. If the United States was to be a global power, the president would need to travel all over the globe. He needed to meet face-to-face with other world leaders.

On January 11, 1943, Roosevelt became the first president to fly while in office. When the Clipper took off with Roosevelt aboard, it changed the job of the president of the United States forever.

was very much like riding in a luxury train of that era—except that the Clipper was going almost 200 miles (322 km) per hour and flying about 10,000 feet (3,048 m) over the ocean's waves. Of course, that level of luxury came at a high price. Round-trip airfare on the Clipper was $675. Today, that would equal about $8,000.

Today, Americans are used to seeing their president fly all over the globe. But for the first 120 years of the presidency, presidents of the United States stayed close to home. None of the first twenty-five presidents left the United States while they were in office. They were expected to remain on American soil and tend to business at home. Theodore Roosevelt (a distant cousin of Franklin Roosevelt who served as president from 1901 to 1909) changed that when he visited Panama in 1906. He became the first president to travel overseas. He went by steamship.

It's easy to understand why Theodore Roosevelt traveled by ship. It had been only three years since Wilbur and Orville Wright's first-ever airplane flight in 1903. Air travel was still very risky. Keeping a plane in the air for more than a few minutes was considered an accomplishment.

However, by the 1940s, great advances had been made in air travel. Planes circled the globe. They made it possible for travelers to cross continents and oceans much more quickly than they could in trains or ships.

World politics was changing, as well. During World War II, the United States stepped forward as one of the great powers of the world. By the 1940s, the president of the United States could no longer afford to stay at home. As the leader of a world power, he had to be ready to travel the world.

Franklin Roosevelt's successful trip to North Africa with pilot Howard Cone showed how important air travel could be for the president. In the North African city of Casablanca, Roosevelt and Churchill were able to make plans for an Allied invasion of Europe that helped win World War II.

Roosevelt (back left) celebrates his sixty-first birthday while flying home from the Casablanca conference. Howard Cone (front right) joins the party.

The historic flight was not an easy one, though. To reach Casablanca, Roosevelt and the Clipper flying boat had to fly for more than three days. Today, that trip would take about seven hours. Roosevelt's Clipper carried few luxury items. One berth was equipped with a double mattress. Some extra towels and a few extra chairs were put aboard. To make it look like any other military plane, the Clipper even wore standard camouflage paint.

Roosevelt's difficult trip aboard the Clipper had far-reaching consequences. It showed that the president could travel the globe safely, even in wartime, going wherever he needed. Air travel gave the president of the United States the freedom and mobility to be a world leader.

It wasn't long before every president of the United States had an airplane to call his own. Today we call that plane *Air Force One*.

THE PRESIDENT'S PLANE

IT STANDS AS TALL as a five-story building. It flies at more than 600 miles (966 km) per hour. Its high-tech defenses can fight off missile attacks. It is the most famous plane in the world. The plane is *Air Force One*, and it carries the president of the United States.

Today's *Air Force One* marks a great technological advance from the days of Roosevelt's flight on the Clipper. But the mission is the same: to take the president wherever he needs to go, at a moment's notice, anywhere in the world. On *Air Force One*, the president can fly around the world for meetings with other heads of state. Or he can make a quick trip home for a weekend of rest away from the White House. Whatever the destination, *Air Force One* stands ready to take him.

"Air Force One" is the call sign, or code name, for any Air Force plane flying the president of the United States. As soon as the president steps on board any Air Force plane, that plane becomes *Air Force One*. The president usually flies on one of two identical airplanes that are set aside for his use. They are a part of what the Air Force calls the presidential air transport fleet.

Both planes wear identical paint jobs that identify them as the president's plane. On the tail of the planes is painted an American flag. Near the nose of

Air Force One *is always ready and waiting at Andrews Air Force Base in Maryland to take the president anywhere he needs to go.*

The presidential seal decorates the plane. It is an important symbol of the U.S. presidency.

the planes is the Seal of the President of the United States, an image of an eagle surrounded by a circle of stars. The bold lettering across the body of the planes spells out: "United States of America." When *Air Force One* touches down on a runway anywhere in the world, those markings announce to the world that the president of the United States has arrived. Like the White House, *Air Force One* is a symbol of the presidency.

In fact, *Air Force One* is like a flying White House. Just about any job the president can do in the White House, he can do on board his planes. From his chair behind his large desk, he can conduct meetings, write letters, or read. He can use one of the eighty-five telephones on *Air Force One* to call anywhere in the world. He can even talk to the commander of a submarine deep below the ocean—from 30,000 feet (9,144 m) above Earth.

Of course, the president is not the only one at work on *Air Force One*. The plane also has workstations for the president's staff and for reporters who travel

The president's office onboard Air Force One *is a fully equipped workstation where he can conduct meetings and do just about any presidential task necessary. Here, President Bill Clinton is consulted during a meeting aboard* Air Force One.

with him. *Air Force One* is equipped with televisions, computers, fax machines, and photocopiers. Almost 240 miles (386 km) of wire snake through the plane.

When he's not working, the president can relax in the rooms provided for him and his family. There's a bedroom with two foldout beds for the president and first lady. There are twin bathrooms with showers. And there's a sitting room, for meeting with guests. The president can even choose a movie from the video library on board.

At mealtime, *Air Force One* has two kitchens—or galleys, as they are called on planes and ships—equipped to prepare plenty of food. The plane can store enough food in its pantries and freezers for two thousand meals. All meals are served on plates bearing the presidential seal.

President George H. W. Bush tours the galley of the aircraft, where all the meals are carefully prepared. The two galleys are equipped to prepare one hundred meals at a time.

Air Force One is a military plane, so it also comes equipped with advanced defense capabilities. Its electrical systems are protected so that they would continue working even through a nuclear bomb blast. Inside the plane is a hospital room with an operating table and lifesaving equipment, in case of an emergency. It also carries top-secret defensive systems to fend off missile attacks. To maintain the president's safety, the Air Force will not disclose details of these defenses.

In addition, *Air Force One* includes seating for seventy-six passengers and twenty-six crew members. It takes a huge plane to hold all this. In fact, *Air Force One* is one of the largest passenger planes flying. It measures more than 231 feet (70 m) long. That's nearly the length of a football field. *Air Force One*

There are workstations on Air Force One *for the president's staff and for reporters.*

AIR FORCE ONE FACTS AND FIGURES

Height: 63 feet, 5 inches (19.3 m)
Length: 231 feet, 10 inches (70.7 m)
Wingspan: 195 feet, 8 inches (59.6 m)
Weight: more than 400 tons

Speed: 630 miles (1,014 km) per hour
Home base: 89th Airlift Wing, Andrews Air Force Base, Maryland

is a 747, just like many of the airplanes used by everyday air travelers. Of course, those planes don't have the special features found on the president's planes.

But there's a bigger difference between *Air Force One* and ordinary airplanes. *Air Force One* is a flying symbol of the United States. There are other symbols of the United States, such as the Capitol, the White House, and the Statue of Liberty. Travelers come from all over the world to visit these places because they represent American democracy. But *Air Force One* is the only national symbol that travels around the world. Wherever it goes, *Air Force One* represents the United States and its president.

THE SACRED COW

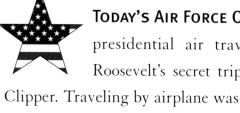

TODAY'S AIR FORCE ONE is just the latest chapter in the history of presidential air travel. That history began with Franklin Roosevelt's secret trip to North Africa aboard Howard Cone's Clipper. Traveling by airplane was difficult for Franklin Roosevelt. Unable to walk since being stricken with polio in 1921, he used a wheelchair. That made just getting on an airplane hard. He had to be carried onto the Clipper for his

THE PLANE THAT WOULD HAVE CARRIED THE PRESIDENT

The first plane assigned to the president of the United States never flew with a president on board. It was named the *Guess Where II*, and in 1943 and 1944 it stood ready to transport Franklin Roosevelt. (It would be another fifteen years or so before the name "Air Force One" was coined.) The *Guess Where II* was a modified B-24 bomber, a kind of plane flight to Africa in 1943. Once he was on board, moving around the narrow cabin was difficult, too. Airplanes of the 1940s were not designed for people in wheelchairs.

So in 1943, the Army Air Corps had a plane made especially for Roosevelt. It was a version of a C-54 Skymaster transport plane—a kind of plane usually used to carry troops and supplies for the military. But this plane was loaded with features that made it different from any other C-54. Most of these features were produced to meet the president's special needs.

Roosevelt grew bored on long plane trips. He liked to move around and visit with other passengers. He liked to sit in the cockpit and watch the pilots work. So the designers of his new plane produced a special portable wheelchair that allowed him to move freely around the cabin. Even boarding this plane would be easier for Roosevelt. To board other planes, the president had to be rolled up long ramps in his wheelchair. His new plane came with an elevator that simply lifted the president from the ground into the plane's cabin.

On board his new plane was everything the president would need on long trips. The president was provided with an office desk, a swivel chair, and a telephone that allowed him to speak with the plane's pilots in the cockpit. A large sofa could be turned into a bed. A large bulletproof window near the president's desk allowed him to enjoy the view.

A B-24 bomber

used for long-distance bombing missions during World War II. These bombers were one of the most effective weapons of World War II for the United States. But Army Air Force officials began receiving reports of safety problems on similar planes and feared the *Guess Where II* wasn't safe enough for the president of the United States. As a result, Roosevelt never flew on the *Guess Where II*.

17 ★

The Sacred Cow *was the first military aircraft to transport a president.*

Army Air Force officials thought that such an airplane deserved a grand name. They wanted to call the plane the "Flying White House." However, reporters named it the *Sacred Cow*, and that name stuck. The *Sacred Cow* was completed in 1944. Today, it looks old-fashioned compared with the modern *Air Force One*. Today's *Air Force One* can fly more than twice as fast as the *Sacred Cow*. Today's plane is more than twice as long, as well. But the *Sacred Cow* was one of the most advanced planes of its time.

In February 1945, the *Sacred Cow* carried Roosevelt to another important overseas meeting. It flew Roosevelt to Yalta for the last of his wartime conferences with British prime minister Winston Churchill and Soviet leader Joseph Stalin. There the three leaders discussed plans for rebuilding Europe after World War II. It was the only time that Roosevelt would fly on the plane designed for him. Two months later, he died at his vacation home in Georgia.

HARRY TRUMAN'S INDEPENDENCE

 UPON ROOSEVELT'S DEATH, Harry Truman (1945–1953) became the thirty-third president of the United States. Truman also inherited the *Sacred Cow*, the plane designed for Franklin Roosevelt.

Truman wasted no time putting the plane to work. He made his first presidential flight only three weeks after taking office. The *Sacred Cow* flew Truman to his hometown of Independence, Missouri, for a one-day visit. It was the first flight made by a president within the United States. It was also the first of Truman's many flights in office.

Like Roosevelt, Truman used the *Sacred Cow* to travel to meetings with leaders all over the world. In June 1945, he flew to San Francisco to attend the meeting that formed the United Nations. In July, the *Sacred Cow* flew him part of the way to Potsdam, Germany. There he met with British leaders and Soviet leader Joseph Stalin as part of the ongoing series of meetings between Allied heads of state.

But unlike Roosevelt, Truman also used the *Sacred Cow* for short vacations. To Truman, the president's plane was a refuge where he could escape the pressures of his job for a few hours. Truman was sometimes criticized by reporters for his frequent travel. On Christmas Day 1945, he flew home to Independence to have Christmas dinner at home with his family. The plane had to fly through snowstorms to get to Independence. Some newspaper accounts claimed that the president had needlessly put himself in danger.

But that didn't stop Truman from enjoying the presidential plane. He even used the plane to play practical jokes. On May 19, 1946, Truman was planning to fly home to Independence once more to visit his mother. Truman's wife, Bess, and his daughter, Margaret, stayed in Washington to attend an air show. Truman knew they would be sitting on the roof of the White House watching the planes' maneuvers. So, on the way to Missouri, he asked the pilot of the *Sacred Cow* to fly low over the White House. He wanted to wave at his wife and daughter from the window of the plane. The pilot did just that, passing over the White House twice at just 500 feet (152 m) above the ground. That was close enough for the president to see the look of surprise on the faces of his wife and daughter as the *Sacred Cow* buzzed past.

After three years of service to two presidents, the *Sacred Cow* was replaced by a new plane. In July 4, 1947, the *Independence* became the official aircraft of the president. The plane was named for Truman's hometown. It was the first presidential plane to look presidential. During World War II, the *Sacred Cow*

BIRTHPLACE OF THE AIR FORCE

The presidential plane *Sacred Cow* was the birthplace of the U. S. Air Force. Harry Truman signed into law the National Security Act on July 26, 1947, while on board the plane. Among other things, the act established the Air Force as an independent service. Before 1947, it had been a branch of the U. S. Army.

had been painted like any other military plane, so that enemy attackers would not know it belonged to the president. Now with the war over, the *Independence* was given a unique paint job. Air Force planners had it painted to look like a fierce eagle, complete with a beak, tail feathers, and cockpit windows where the eagle's eyes would be.

The *Independence* was a Douglas DC-6, a kind of plane used by passenger airlines in the 1950s and 1960s. Of course, like the other presidential planes, the *Independence* had special added features: office space, a desk, and a sofa that could be turned into a bed. It served Truman until 1953. That year, a new president took office. He would soon get a new presidential plane.

The Independence *at Wake Island, a territory of the United States, during what is considered to be the plane's most historic trip. President Truman flew there in 1950 to discuss Korea with General Douglas MacArthur.*

DWIGHT EISENHOWER'S COLUMBINE

 DWIGHT EISENHOWER (1953–1961) was the first president of the United States to have been trained as a pilot. Early in his career in the U. S. Army, he had learned to fly small planes. His wife, Mamie, did not share his interest in air travel. In fact, she was afraid of flying. To make her feel more at home on the new presidential plane, Eisenhower named it the *Columbine*. The columbine is the state flower of Colorado, Mamie Eisenhower's adopted home state. The president's plane featured a painting of an arrangement of blue and white columbines near the nose of the plane.

Eisenhower enjoyed flying, but he was all business on board his planes. He kept a favorite tweed jacket on board for wearing during flights. Before take-off, he took his seat, buckled his seat belt, and followed all the rules of safety. Unlike Truman and Roosevelt, he was not likely to roam the plane, chatting with passengers and the pilot.

Eisenhower flew in three different planes named *Columbine*. All three were Lockheed Constellations, a kind of plane used by commercial airlines in the 1950s. They featured a long, thin body and three rudders on the tail section.

Columbine III had the most advanced communications equipment yet on a presidential plane. Eisenhower was the first president able to speak on the telephone from his airplane with someone on the ground. The *Columbine III* was also the fastest presidential plane. It could fly 330 miles (531 km) per hour. The *Columbine III* served as the president's plane for six years, from 1954 to 1960. By that time, presidential aviation was ready to enter a new era.

INTO THE JET AGE

IN 1959, EISENHOWER BECAME the first president to fly by jet airplane. Up to that time, all presidents had flown on planes driven by propellers. But in the 1950s, more airlines began using planes with jet engines for long flights. Jets had clear advantages over propeller planes. Jet engines allow planes to travel longer distances at higher speeds. Jets also run more smoothly and provide a more comfortable ride for passengers.

Jet engines work by drawing in air and combining it with fuel. This produces a stream of powerful gases that spins a kind of wheel called a turbine. The turbine makes all the parts of the jet engine run.

The first presidential jet was a Boeing 707, a kind of plane already in use by many airlines. In late 1959, a 707 took Eisenhower on the longest presidential trip yet. He visited eleven countries in eighteen days in the winter of 1959. He touched down in Italy, Turkey, Pakistan, Afghanistan, India, Iran, Greece, Tunisia, France, Spain, and Morocco.

A Boeing 707 was the first kind of jet airplane flown by a president in 1959. These planes were already being used by many airlines.

HOW AIR FORCE ONE GOT ITS NAME

The name "Air Force One" was introduced as a radio code name for the president's plane in 1952. All planes are assigned call signs, or code names, to identify them in radio communications with other planes and with air traffic controllers. The name "Air Force One" was meant to prevent confusing the president's plane with another, ordinary plane.

JOHN KENNEDY AND THE NEW LOOK OF AIR FORCE ONE

 THE AIR FORCE CAME UP WITH the new code name for the president's plane. But it was John Kennedy (1961–1963) who helped make the name famous around the world.

In 1962, Kennedy took delivery of a new jet plane, the first to be designed exclusively for the president. It could fly 1,000 miles (1,609 km) farther without stopping to refuel than previous presidential planes. It could fly 550 miles (885 km) per hour—almost twice as fast as *Columbine II*. It was a modified Boeing 707, like the plane that Eisenhower flew in 1959. But Kennedy's plane looked different. The new president asked designer Raymond Loewy to give the plane a sharp new image. Loewy came up with the blue-and-white color scheme that is still in use on the president's planes.

When Kennedy wasn't on board, the Air Force called the plane SAM 26000. "SAM" stands for Special Air Missions, a branch of the Air Force that provided transport for high-ranking government and military leaders. The number 26000 was the plane's tail number—the identification number painted on the tail of the plane. But Kennedy's worldwide travels made the plane

The president's plane is not the only vehicle with such a code name. Any Marine helicopter that carries the president is called *Marine One*. If the president travels by Navy ship, that ship is called *Navy One*. Any Air Force plane carrying the vice president is assigned the code name *Air Force Two*.

famous under a different name. All around the world, people learned to call the plane *Air Force One*.

In June 1963, Kennedy flew *Air Force One* to Berlin. At the time, Berlin was a divided city. West Berlin was controlled by the United States and its allies. East Berlin was under the iron-fisted rule of the Soviet Union. The two sections of the city were divided by a wall built in 1961. It was designed to keep

President Kennedy and the first lady, Jacqueline Kennedy, after their first flight in the brand-new Air Force One *jet plane. This new color scheme on the plane is still used by* Air Force One *today.*

East Berliners from escaping to freedom. In a public square in Berlin, Kennedy delivered a historic speech to thousands of people gathered in a city plaza, promising that the freedom-loving countries of the world would not abandon them. "I am a Berliner," he declared in German to the crowd. The Berliners cheered wildly.

AIR FORCE ONE AND A DAY OF TRAGEDY

 LATE IN 1963, *Air Force One* took Kennedy on a series of trips around the United States. He was beginning his campaign for reelection in 1964. One of those campaign trips was to Dallas, Texas, on November 22, 1963. Driving through Dallas in an open car that day, Kennedy was shot and killed by an assassin. With Kennedy's death, Vice President Lyndon Johnson automatically became president. Johnson was in Dallas with Kennedy that day, and immediately Secret Service agents had to get Johnson to a safe place. They rushed him back to the airport and *Air Force One*.

With Mrs. Kennedy looking on, Johnson took the presidential oath of office on board *Air Force One*. Then the president's plane carried Johnson, Mrs. Kennedy, and dozens of others back to the nation's capital. In the back of the plane was the flag-draped casket holding the body of John Kennedy.

Three days later, Kennedy's body was laid to rest at Arlington National Cemetery outside Washington, D.C. During the ceremony, pilots flew *Air Force One* over the cemetery. They dipped the plane's wings in one final salute to the fallen president.

LYNDON JOHNSON'S THRONE

 AS KENNEDY'S SUCCESSOR, Lyndon Johnson (1963–1969) began his presidency on board *Air Force One*. The plane became one of his favorite places to entertain guests. He had his crew keep the plane stocked with plenty of big steaks and cold root beer. He had all the seats on the plane turned around so they faced his office. And he had a roomy new office chair installed for himself. It came with a switch that allowed the president to raise the chair so he would always be sitting taller than anyone else on the plane. Johnson's staff called it the throne.

On board Air Force One, *Vice President Lyndon Johnson takes the oath to become thirty-sixth president of the United States after the assassination of President John Kennedy. On the left is Johnson's wife, Lady Bird Johnson, and on the right is Jacqueline Kennedy, the widow of President Kennedy.*

President Johnson in the chair his staff called the throne, which was raised higher than the rest of the seats on the plane.

During Johnson's five years in office, the plane carried him all over the world. In 1967, Johnson and *Air Force One* set a presidential long-distance travel record. He flew more than 28,000 miles (45,060 km) in five days, visiting Australia, Thailand, Vietnam, Pakistan, and Italy. But his favorite destination was his ranch in his home state of Texas. Johnson enjoyed *Air Force One* so much that he took many of the plane's contents with him when he left office. His staff removed not only his "throne" office chair but also towels, drinking glasses, and other souvenirs bearing the *Air Force One* logo.

PRESIDENTIAL MENUS

The crew members of *Air Force One* get to know the favorite foods of their presidential passengers. John Kennedy liked to relax with a bowl of chowder. Lyndon Johnson preferred steak. Richard Nixon and Gerald Ford both liked cottage cheese. Of course, the

RICHARD NIXON'S FINAL FLIGHT

 THE SAME PLANE ALSO SERVED Richard Nixon (1969–1974) in the first four years of his presidency. Like Johnson, he flew *Air Force One* all over the world. Just one month into his presidency, he flew to Vietnam to visit American troops stationed there during the Vietnam War. In July 1969, he flew to Hawaii to meet the astronauts of the Apollo 11 space mission, just back from the first moon landing. In 1972, he flew to China, becoming the first U.S. president to visit that country.

All those air miles took their toll on SAM 26000, the plane that became *Air Force One* when the president boarded. In 1972, it was replaced by an identical plane. The new plane was given the tail number SAM 27000, and it served Nixon for the last two years of his presidency.

On August 9, 1974, Nixon became the first president to resign his office. He had been accused of breaking laws to cover up crimes committed by his staff members. That day he boarded *Air Force One* for his last flight in office. As president, he had visited more countries and traveled more miles than any other president. Now he was returning to his home in California.

In Washington, Vice President Gerald Ford was preparing to take Nixon's place as president. At noon, he took the presidential oath of office.

crew also learns what presidents don't like to eat. George H.W. Bush made no secret of the fact that he couldn't stand broccoli. So the crew declared *Air Force One* a broccoli-free zone. They even hung a NO BROCCOLI sign outside the plane's galley.

Nixon and his staff listened to the ceremony on an *Air Force One* radio, flying 40,000 feet (12,192 m) over Jefferson City, Missouri. Once Ford was officially in office, the pilot of *Air Force One* contacted air traffic control in Kansas City. "Kansas City, this was *Air Force One*," he said. "Will you change our call sign to SAM 27000?" For the rest of the trip, the plane was called SAM 27000. Richard Nixon was no longer the president flying on *Air Force One*. He was a private citizen traveling on the president's plane.

THE HISTORIC FLIGHTS OF SAM 27000

 SAM 27000 CONTINUED TO SERVE as the presidential plane until 1990. It was the plane that Gerald Ford (1974–1977) flew to Salzburg, Austria, in 1975. At the airport in Salzburg, Ford stumbled and fell down a flight of stairs exiting the plane. For the rest of his presidency, he was stuck with a reputation for clumsiness.

Jimmy Carter (1977–1981) was so excited about his first ride on *Air Force One* that he nearly left without an important passenger—his mother. At the last minute, a limousine brought Mrs. Carter to the airport.

Gerald Ford's famous fall while leaving Air Force One

During Carter's presidency, fifty-two Americans working at the U.S. embassy in Iran were held hostage for fourteen months by Iranian student revolutionaries. Carter worked hard to win their release, but the hostages were not freed until the day he left office. His successor, Ronald Reagan, asked Carter to fly to Germany to meet the freed hostages. He loaned him *Air Force One*.

Reagan (1981–1989) flew the same plane to Germany in 1987. There he demanded that Soviet leader Mikhail Gorbachev tear down the wall dividing East Berlin from West Berlin. Within two years, the Berlin Wall was indeed torn down.

TWIN PRESIDENTIAL PLANES

DURING REAGAN'S PRESIDENCY, plans were made for a new kind of presidential plane. The existing *Air Force One* was aging. There was no room on board for new advanced communications equipment. And the airline industry was building new planes that could fly farther and faster than *Air Force One.*

The U.S. government spent $650 million building two identical new planes to serve as *Air Force One.* They were Boeing 747s, the largest passenger planes flying. They were completed in 1990 and 1991, and given the tail numbers 28000 and 29000. The first president to fly in the new planes was George H.W. Bush (1989–1993). Amazed at the size and advanced technology of the new planes, Bush said the difference between the new presidential planes and the old planes was "like night and day."

PRESIDENTIAL PRIVILEGES

Presidents enjoy special treatment on board *Air Force One*, but they can also be criticized for abusing their privileges. In 1993, Bill Clinton caused a stir when he had *Air Force One* wait on a runway at Los Angeles International Airport while a Los Angeles hair stylist cut his hair on the plane. Other airplanes at the airport were waiting for *Air Force One* to take off, so Clinton's haircut ended up causing delays for other air travelers. Clinton was criticized for putting himself ahead of American travelers.

Presidents can relax aboard Air Force One. *President Reagan found time to work on his putting.*

The twin planes also served Bill Clinton (1993–2001) and George W. Bush (2001–). In 1995, *Air Force One* carried Clinton and former presidents George H.W. Bush and Jimmy Carter to Israel for the funeral of Israeli prime minister Yitzhak Rabin. Even former presidents had to find their own sleeping space on the crowded plane. On the return trip, Carter and Bush stretched out on the floor of the cabin to catch a few hours of sleep.

Also on board for the trip was Newt Gingrich, speaker of the House of Representatives. At the time, Gingrich and Clinton were trying to reach agreement on the president's proposed budget for the federal government. Partly because he was upset at being assigned a seat in the rear of the plane, Gingrich resolved to block congressional approval of Clinton's budget. The result was a twenty-two-day partial shutdown of the government. The shutdown left thousands of federal workers without paychecks for weeks and delayed government payments to poor people and disabled veterans.

A brand-new Air Force One *747 rolls out of the paint hangar at Boeing in 1990.*

AIR FORCE ONE AND A DAY OF TERROR

ON SEPTEMBER 11, 2001, terrorists hijacked four passenger airplanes and killed thousands in attacks on New York City and Washington, D.C. As the day's terrible events unfolded, *Air Force One* played a key role in keeping President George W. Bush safe.

The president was speaking to children at a Florida grade school when the first of the attacks occurred in New York City. After making a brief statement on television from the school, he boarded *Air Force One*. His Secret Service protectors warned the president that terrorists might be planning to attack *Air Force One* or sites in Washington, D.C. So instead of returning to Washington, *Air Force One* and the president headed first for an Air Force base in Louisiana. After a brief stop there, the plane flew to another Air Force base, in Nebraska.

As the plane flew, it was accompanied by Air Force fighter jets. They were prepared to protect the plane in case of attack. At the same time, the plane's advanced communications equipment allowed the president to keep pace with the rapidly unfolding events of the day, and to direct his administration's

After the terrorist attacks of September 11, 2001, Air Force One security was greatly increased. Here, bomb technicians and bomb-sniffing dogs check the baggage that is about to be loaded onto the plane.

39 ★

On September 11, F-16 fighter jets accompanied Air Force One *in order to protect the plane against possible terrorist attacks.*

response. Finally, about eight hours after the first attack, *Air Force One* returned the president safely to Andrews Air Force Base in Maryland, the home of *Air Force One*. From there, he was flown in his *Marine One* helicopter to the White House grounds. The sight of the president walking safely off the helicopter and returning to his home reassured a tense nation.

Facing page: Marine One *helicopter lifting off from the south lawn of the White House*

41 ★

AIR FORCE ONE TODAY

THE TWIN PRESIDENTIAL PLANES rest in a huge hangar at Andrews Air Force Base in Maryland. The base is just 10 miles (16 km) from the White House, which means that the president can get there in minutes in his *Marine One* helicopter. When he arrives at the base, he always finds his plane ready to fly. Keeping the planes ready is the job of the 89th Airlift Wing of the U. S. Air Force, which maintains the presidential air fleet. The 89th is made up of more than 160 flight engineers, pilots, flight attendants, communications specialists, security staff, and others. Each time *Air Force One* flies, it carries a crew of twenty-six. Each member of the crew is selected from the best talent in the Air Force.

Planning a presidential trip involves many more people. Most presidential flights are the result of long and careful planning. In fact, each trip is officially considered a military operation. Planning is led by the White House Military Office. It works with the Secret Service; the Federal Bureau of Investigation; local police; and the Army, Navy, Air Force, Marines, and Coast Guard to make sure each trip goes smoothly.

Long before the president is ready to fly, the members of the 89th Airlift Wing prepare *Air Force One*. Mechanics and engineers work in pairs to ensure

AT THE CONTROLS

Air Force One's pilots are among the Air Force's best. To qualify, pilots must have spent at least two thousand hours flying, be qualified as pilot instructors, and have a spotless record.

that repair work is done properly. Maintenance crews slip on cotton booties inside the plane to keep the wall-to-wall carpeting clean. No one is allowed to enter *Air Force One*'s hangar without passing security checkpoints.

Even the kitchen staff of *Air Force One* take great care in their preparations. They go shopping for the food that will be served on *Air Force One* at a different grocery store for each trip. This way they make sure that no one is able to tamper with the food.

As the time set for *Air Force One*'s departure nears, the preparations continue. The runway at Andrews Air Force Base is carefully inspected for any debris that would interfere with the plane's takeoff and ruin *Air Force One*'s perfect safety record. The airplane's fuel is tested, then the fuel tank is sealed to prevent tampering. Fire trucks and ambulances stand by in case of an emergency. Bulletproof limousines are loaded onto cargo planes for use at the president's destination.

About twenty minutes before takeoff, the president begins heading toward Andrews Air Force Base in *Marine One*. The base goes into "lockdown," its highest level of security. When the president arrives, his plane is ready for takeoff. Once he boards the plane, the crew is notified: "The president is on board, and we are *Air Force One*." Inside, the president finds spotless carpets, roomy chairs, and comfortable sofas. Desks and tables are polished until they are gleaming. Draped over his office chair is an *Air Force One* flight jacket, a windbreaker with his name inscribed over the left pocket.

Air Force One has seventy-six seats, with separate sections for the president's staff, security personnel, important guests of the president, and members of the press. On a typical trip, dozens of people fly with the president. Advisers, speechwriters, assistants, and other White House staff travel with the president. So do hundreds of reporters, photographers, and camera operators. Only a few travel on *Air Force One*, however. The rest follow on another plane.

The reporters flying on *Air Force One* are called the press pool. The pool changes for every trip. The members of the pool must share news they obtain with the rest of the press covering the president. They are also required to stay in the back of the plane.

On some trips the president will invite members of Congress or foreign leaders to fly with him. Presidents know that a ride on *Air Force One* will impress even the most important political figure. If the president wants to win the support of a member of Congress, *Air Force One* can be a great tool for making friends and influencing people.

There is one more important passenger on every presidential flight—the big briefcase containing the codes that allow the president to launch nuclear weapons. It is placed in a safe inside *Air Force One* as soon as the president boards the plane, and it stays there throughout the flight.

Most Americans will never get to see the inside of *Air Force One*. Most will never see all the activity that goes into planning a presidential flight. But many of us have seen the familiar image of the president stepping off *Air Force One*

Ceremonies usually mark the president's arrival overseas. A military guard welcomed George W. Bush and Laura Bush to Ljubljana in Slovenia.

at the end of a flight. We have seen the president stop at the top of the stairs to wave to the gathered crowd. We have seen him stop at the bottom of the stairs to salute his military guards. Every time that scene plays out, it means that *Air Force One* has successfully delivered its most important passenger.

The president's planes have evolved from the propeller planes of the 1940s to today's jumbo jets. Today's twin presidential planes are 231 feet (70 m) long. That's longer than the distance the Wright Brothers flew on their first flight in 1903. Whatever their size, the president's planes have been ambassadors for America. They have brought the ideals and the power of the United States to people all over the world.

Air Force One *is always proudly welcomed as a symbol of the United States.*

WHERE TO SEE HISTORIC PRESIDENTIAL PLANES

Museum of Flight
8404 East Marginal Way South
Seattle, Washington 98108
206-764-5700
The Museum of Flight is home to the first presidential jet aircraft, a Boeing 707 that was introduced in 1959. It was used by presidents Eisenhower and Kennedy.

Ronald Reagan Presidential Library and Museum
40 Presidential Drive
Simi Valley, California 93065
800-410-8354
The Reagan Library is home to SAM 27000, a 707 that was used by seven presidents, beginning with Richard Nixon. It was used for the last time by George W. Bush in 2001.

United States Air Force Museum
1100 Spaatz Street
Wright-Patterson Air Force Base, Ohio 45435
937-255-3286
The United States Air Force Museum displays nine presidential aircraft, including Franklin Roosevelt's *Sacred Cow*, Harry Truman's *Independence*, Dwight D. Eisenhower's *Columbine III*, and SAM 26000, the 707 that flew eight different presidents.

TO LEARN MORE

VIDEO

National Geographic: *Air Force One*, 2001.
A behind-the-scenes look at life aboard the president's plane, this video takes viewers along on a typical presidential flight and includes interviews with former presidents.

WEB SITES

Boeing's *Air Force One*
www.boeing.com/defense-space/military/af1/
Technical and historic background on *Air Force One* from Boeing, the Chicago-based company that built the president's planes.

United States Air Force Museum Presidential Aircraft Gallery
www.wpafb.af.mil/museum/annex/ans.htm
Details on presidents' planes of the past, from *Sacred Cow* to SAM 26000.